My dedication to this sacred duty

is total and whole-hearted.

In the responsibility bestowed on me

never will I falter.

And with dignity and perseverance

my standard will remain perfection.

Through the years of diligence and praise

and the discomfort of the elements,

I will walk my tour in humble reverence

to the best of my ability.

It is he who commands the respect I protect,

his bravery that made us so proud.

Surrounded by well meaning crowds by day,

alone in the thoughtful peace of night,

this soldier will in honored glory rest

under my eternal vigilance.

—THE SENTINEL'S CREED

TWENTY-ONE STEPS

Guarding the Tomb of the Unknown Soldier

JEFF GOTTESFELD

illustrated by MATT TAVARES

CANDLEWICK PRESS

I am an Unknown. I am one of many.

We fell for the last time in the Argonne Forest.
At Somme. Belleau Wood.
Facedown in trenches,
faceup on hillsides.
We fell a thousand ways.

In life, we were our mothers' sons.
In death, we are faded photos on the mantel,
empty chairs at Thanksgiving,
prayers in the dark before dawn.
We are known but to God.

After the War to End All Wars, most of America's fallen came home. Their families could place flowers on their graves and pebbles on their headstones. But combat's vile fury left others nameless and faceless. There was no way for loved ones to claim us, no place for our nation to honor our sacrifice.

In 1921, one unknown returned to stand for all. I was transported by the navy to Washington and lay in state in the Capitol, where an army of mourners filed past my casket. Many were families whose sons died nameless and faceless. As they knelt, prayed, and anointed my flag with tears, I felt their stories. The stories of a Boston kid who swung for the fences, a Texas boy who broke horses, a Choctaw Nation farmhand, a Nevada miner.

In that moment, I became theirs.

On the eleventh day of the eleventh month, at the eleventh hour, a team of horses bore me to Arlington. Thousands packed the amphitheater. There were speeches, Taps, and a twenty-one gun salute when I was laid to rest. As the day lengthened, those for whom I died lingered and drifted on the roiled waters of loss. I gave them peace.

People, though, forget easily. My tomb stands on a hillcrest. It did
not take long for visitors to come for the view and not the meaning.
Some brought picnics, feasting gaily above my bones.

Volunteers put a stop to that desecration. But as the plaza emptied in
the gloaming, I lay alone with my war: mustard gas and barbed wire,
bayonet charges, and names unanswered at roll call.

Late one half-moon night,
I heard footsteps.

The sharp *click* of heels. Silence.

Another *click*. More silence.

Twenty-one footsteps.

Click.

Twenty-one seconds of silence.

Click.

Twenty-one seconds of silence.

Twenty-one more steps.

With each step, my war was over.

From that moment, I have never been alone again. No matter the hour or the weather, a sentinel guards the plaza. It is the most difficult post to earn in the army. Many fail for each one chosen. Those granted the privilege may walk the mat for two years. Everything they do honors the unknown fallen.

They press their creases sharp as a razor.

Rehem their trousers so they lie just right.

Singe loose threads from their jackets' topstitching.

Space their medals down to ¹⁄₆₄ of an inch.

Practice keeping their forearms at 90 degrees.

Recount pages of cemetery history.

Set their hat brims two fingers above their eyes.

Dampen their gloves to better grip their rifles.

March so their heads stay ever level.

Add metal to their heels for the sharpest click.

Polish their "spits" for hours every day.

The Tomb Guards are men and women of every race, religion, and creed. Before joining the army, they were students, mechanics, and supermarket baggers. They have names, families, and stories.

Once on the mat, they are only Americans.
Their standard is perfection.

My guards were present when more Unknowns came home. One from World War II and one from Korea. Then, years later, one from Vietnam. They lay in state in the Capitol as I did, where an army of mourners filed past the caskets. Many were families whose sons died nameless and faceless. Mothers, fathers, sisters, and brothers knelt, prayed, and anointed the flags with tears. Their stories were different and the same.

In time, through the wonder of science, the Vietnam Unknown was named and returned to his family. His crypt is now empty. We who remain are never alone. Our guards keep faith.

There is admiration in their pants crease.

Duty in their hems.

Focus in their topstitching.

Gratitude between the medals.

Reverence in the angle of their rifles.

Discipline in their learning.

Respect in their hat brims.

Fidelity in their gloves.

Appreciation in their step.

Devotion in their heel clicks.

And love in their gleaming spits.

I am an Unknown. I am one of many. From Bunker Hill to Heartbreak Ridge, we gave all we had for our country and freedom. The Tomb Guards give all they have for us.

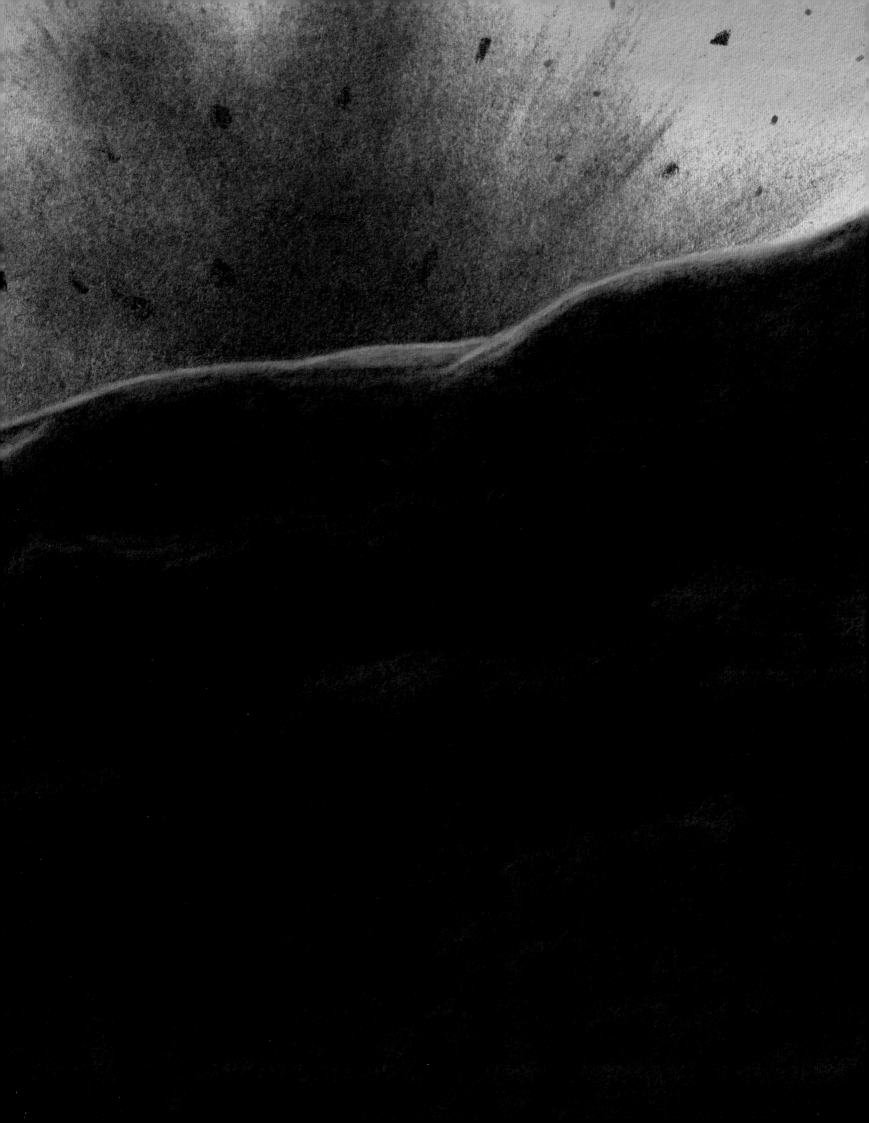

In glorious sunshine, on bluebird days, the plaza shimmers with life. Crowds gather; aging veterans, tourists, and school groups line the marble steps.

They marvel at our sentinels. Then they gaze past the mat to the tomb, and imagine our stories. In that moment, we become theirs.

In wretched night, when stinging sleet makes daybreak a distant dream, the plaza is desolate. Our guards need no audience in their quest for perfection. As they walk the mat, they listen for our voices on the howling wind.

HERE RESTS IN
HONORED GLORY
AN AMERICAN
SOLDIER
KNOWN BUT TO GOD

In snow, in rain.

On days the birds don't dare to sing.

Twenty-one, twenty-one, twenty-one.

By day, by night.

Before many, few, or none.

Twenty-one, twenty-one, twenty-one.

Guard our perfect rest.

Give us now your very best.

Twenty-one. Twenty-one. Twenty-one.

Twenty-one.

AFTERWORD

Arlington National Cemetery is the final resting place for more than 400,000 active duty service members, veterans, and their families. The service members and veterans include those who fought for America going back to the Revolution. Dozens of funerals are conducted there daily. An unidentified soldier from the First World War was interred at the Tomb of the Unknown Soldier on November 11, 1921—Armistice Day, now known as Veterans Day. Unknowns from World War II and the Korean War were interred on Memorial Day, 1958, while the Vietnam Unknown was buried on Memorial Day, 1984. Later identified, he was disinterred in May 1998. The unidentified soldiers interred here represent countless unknowns buried at Arlington, other national cemeteries, and around the world.

The tomb has been guarded around the clock by the Tomb Guard, a special military unit, since midnight on July 2, 1937. Becoming a Tomb Guard sentinel is exceptionally difficult. Guards are devoted to the Sentinel's Creed, which appears at the beginning of this book. The full name of the creed's author is, fittingly, unknown.

The cemetery and tomb are open every day of the year. There is a sentinel on the plaza at every moment. The Unknowns are never alone. This book would have been impossible without the assistance of many Tomb Guards past and present, historians, and organizations, particularly the Society of the Honor Guard, Tomb of the Unknown Soldier.

To the members of the armed forces of the United States of America,
past, present, and future
JG

For the Unknowns
MT

Text copyright © 2021 by Jeff Gottesfeld. Illustrations copyright © 2021 by Matt Tavares. All rights reserved. No part of this book may be reproduced, transmitted, or stored in an information retrieval system in any form or by any means, graphic, electronic, or mechanical, including photocopying, taping, and recording, without prior written permission from the publisher. First edition 2021. Library of Congress Catalog Card Number 2021933330
ISBN 978-1-5362-0148-2. This book was typeset in Adobe Garamond. The illustrations were done in pencil and painted digitally.
Candlewick Press, 99 Dover Street, Somerville, Massachusetts 02144. www.candlewick.com.
Printed in Shenzhen, Guangdong, China. 23 24 25 CCP 10 9 8 7 6 5